365 DAYS OF REAL

David K. Reynolds, I

Foreword

This little book offers reminders for living, one for each day of the year. Daily life has no Foreword or Afterword, only Contents – 365 days a year worth of Contents.

The source of the contents in this book remains a mystery.

Thinking can be a help or a hindrance to proper action. A clear purpose is like a porch light in the darkness. Find your moment's porch light and head straight for it.

You decide what you need to do. No one really knows why you so decide, not even you.

Tales of motivation are elaborate children's fables.

Sometimes what you do seems to make sense to yourself

and others, sometimes not.

You can't eat "cake" or play a "guitar" or drive a "car".
Beware words in any form, including these words.

All words are not equal. All behaviors are not equal. All
purposes are not equal.
Values are not relative because behavior has
consequences.

Minds roll along. What attracts you today may look
trivial tomorrow. Your mind will move beyond these
words. Come, visit us again sometime.

Life is both simple and complex. You don't really decide
what to do; something decides for you, then you make up
a story about deciding for yourself. Sometimes you do
what you don't want to do, and sometimes you don't do
what you want to do. Those want-to-do's are decided for
you, too.
Nevertheless, do what needs doing, not just for your own

convenience. Please consider what is best for others, too. At least request such consideration from whatever does your considering for you.

Something causes you to connect that shape out there with the word "car". That something is not simply your brain or your learning experience. Sometimes the connection is not there. We pretend that the connection is always there. We build our lives on connections that are presumed to be ongoing. Beware of conceptual foolishness. She is not the same person she was a moment ago, or is she?

You can learn a lot about yourself by living in another country. You discover that some of your assumptions are vaporous. You discover that your sense of competence is fragile. You learn that communication is risky. You grow new eyes and ears. You begin to understand your own embeddedness.
And those are just the first steps.

It often pays to know details. It often pays to observe minutely. If you can avoid tangling yourself in minutia you can see more clearly what needs to be done. Generalities and abstractions are escape routes we use every day. Reality is just as it is, but after we have parsed it up and attached all manner of associations to it, we find ourselves miles away from it. We float ourselves on word breezes. We view terrain from conceptual heights. I wonder how this page feels to you and how it would taste.

There is so much I don't know/understand. So much happens that I don't predict/anticipate. Yet Reality keeps emerging. The show goes on. Even the parts beyond me.

A mistake is a happening plus an evaluation. Cats don't make mistakes. When anything happens, even an unusual happening, cats just do something. Flowers don't make mistakes. Flowers just are.

Regretting past mistakes may or may not be a mistake according to your evaluation. But regrets and remorse won't get your mail sorted.

Life is full of puzzles. Sometimes we do all the right things and the result is not at all what we hoped for. Sometimes we fail to do what is right and the situation turns out well beyond our desired expectations. No one will ever solve those sorts of puzzles satisfactorily, whatever divine or fateful influence they claim to be the cause. Our hopes and expectations are just as puzzling as the outcomes of our actions.

Talking about a problem is easier than doing something about it. Giving advice is easier than following advice. Giving homework assignments is easier than doing them. Giving a political speech is easier than making a law. Words are both useful and suspect. They can promote wisdom and foolishness, peace and war, order and confusion. Don't say I didn't warn you.

If you seek to get control of your feelings your goal is both impossible and unnecessary. Feelings will happen to you just like the sun appearing behind clouds, just like the clouds themselves. It is better to notice the sky and notice the landscape, too. It is better to take into account what is going on in the sky when deciding to carry an umbrella or not. It is better to recognize the sky's conditions but to do what needs doing anyway. Sometimes we have to fly against the wind, sometimes with it. Sometimes we fly though clouds, sometimes through clear skies. To try to make every day sunny involves fruitless effort. Moreover, the result would be boring even if successful. To believe that every day is cloudy is to miss the moments of sunlight shining through a cloud layer. Season yourself with a variety of feelings and behaviors.

One sort of neurotic mind is hyperactive. It adds meaning, interpretations, and associations to all kinds of experience. Sometimes this busyness is useful, often not. Slow your mind down with meditation or keep it busy with constructive, positive topics. Reality is simpler than you think.

Feeling pressured by others, by time, by circumstances is just another feeling. The feeling causes you trouble when you believe you must respond to it or fight it or remove it. Just feel the pressure and continue doing what you need to do.

Some people are tied down by their expectations, standards, pride, status, affiliations, and habits. They knot their mental bonds with flimsy fantasy but never test their holding power. Freedom is just around action's corner. There is no need to decide to break free, no need to motivate yourself, no need to feel ready to change. Doing right is good enough.

Some people become obsessed with fixing themselves, curing themselves, improving themselves, educating themselves, succeeding at business, finding a life partner, finding happiness, achieving respect, gaining control, living comfortably, avoiding aging, and so forth. Obsession narrows the focus of life so that other aspects of life are missed. Goals, objectives, purposes are fine so long as they are realistic and grasped lightly.

Desires will cause you trouble. They will also cause you satisfaction and joy. No one alive eliminates all desires. Everyone alive keeps on breathing. When what you want causes trouble to other people and other creatures and other things, when what you want causes you trouble, then it is time to examine your desires in that area and stop acting on them. The desires are okay, natural. It is the action that must be controlled.

Have you noticed that when you lose yourself in a project you are neither happy nor unhappy? You are just focused, gone. There is something about giving your all in the moment that is (later) quite satisfying. At the time, however, you are so absorbed that your misery and dread and regret are forgotten momentarily. Effort is already good fortune, however the project turns out.

There is something to be said about the phrase "Life is

what you make of it." Your life is actually constructed. What happens is that a lot of stimuli hit your mind, and then your mind makes sense out of all that variety. Your mind somehow knows to pay attention (usually) to what is relevant to you and to ignore (usually) the vast amount of stimuli that are not important to you. How your mind goes about that wondrous feat is still a great mystery. How your mind creates/constructs you is a process that has been examined and debated for more than a thousand years. The good news is that the constructed you has some say in what your mind does. The best way to make your preferences maximized is through purposeful behavior.

We are always changing, always recreated by the ins and outs of Reality. So labels like neurotic or compulsive or obsessed or fearful are only valid some of the time, if at all. Labels make us look static, unchanging. Beware!

Like it or not, Reality happens. Desired or not, feelings occur. Anticipated or not, successes and failures emerge.

Life is like that. So when something gets your attention, attend. When feelings arise, feel them. When successes and failures appear, experience them. Wishing otherwise won't make Reality go away. Learn life's lessons and do what needs doing.

You learn what to call "suffering." You learn what to define as "success" and "failure." Doctors define neurosis. Religious professionals define salvation. Reality is as it is, but you can choose the tags you attach to it. I keep suggesting tags that I have found to be useful. Aim to examine your own tags and make them all realistic.

Stringing words together is our custom. Don't let the strings interfere with the wordless messages of Reality. "I'm addicted", "we are at war", "I could never", "if only I were", "the law says", "you are healed", and the like are strings that may be suspect.

We play games with our minds, or vice versa. There are

social games and religious games and philosophical games and governmental games and legal games and economic games and psychological games and many others. Recognize games as such and play or don't play. Your play determines what kind of player you are and vice versa. Can you see the play here?

There is a lot I don't know. It appears that there is a lot that is truly unknowable. But I don't know that for sure. I'm unsure about certainties. And I'm unsure about my uncertainty. So I doubt my doubts about doubting. And so forth. Finally, I give up and do the best I can (whatever that means).

If your goal is to fix your mind, how do you go about it? In the positive process of fixing it, is it already fixed? How can a broken mind decide to fix itself? Who, then, actually decides to fix your mind? Is it actually possible? Why is it necessary? My mind is becoming tired of all these questions. Maybe it is all right as it is.

We are all humans. No one is more worthy of Reality's recognition than anyone else. No matter what nationality or social status or educational level or religion or degree of wealth or fame, we all reflect Reality's venue. Our value to other humans is determined by what we do, not by how much we know or to whom we were born or how well known we become. Understanding these words doesn't inflate our worth at all.

Do you suffer as you puzzle over these words? Where does your misery go when you lose yourself in washing a car or mowing a lawn or putting on makeup? Misery doesn't lurk somewhere waiting to appear. When it is gone, it is gone. We can, of course, give it the opportunity to renew an appearance.

What do you see other than sights? What do you hear other than sounds? What do you think other than thoughts? These happenings are all you. These words here now are you, too. How like smoke we are! So changeable.

We are taught to see ourselves as unique individuals, special, set apart. No one else suffers as we do, has all the same insights, and enjoys exactly the same pleasures. Our perspective on life is one-of-a-kind. The Japanese, too, have this individuality, though they take pains to conceal it in many social situations. Americans flaunt it. This inflated self-image causes us unnecessary suffering and incomparable joy. Aiming for a sustained satisfied self takes a lot of effort, and we fail to achieve sustained satisfaction a lot. Occasionally stepping back and watching our solitaire game can produce surprising results.

I trust Reality to keep coming, but not necessarily to benefit me. It just keeps on appearing. After all, that reappearing has been my experience so far. I trust Reality to present more data than I notice and understand, more problems, more solutions. Reality stimulates my questioning mind, providing even the questioning mind itself.

My ideas about my mind and about "me" are given to me. My self-image is a gift. Even the notion that I can influence this self-image is a gift. Who then deserves credit for who I think I am? In what sense do I really have a self-concept?

I distrust diagrams about the mind and mental processes. There are more dimensions, more variables, than can be drawn on a page. You can't illustrate a mind to make it visible. Art is a product, not a map. It is also a source.

Your knowing my name is unimportant. Knowing Constructive Living or sutras or the Bible or the Koran is unimportant in comparison with what you do. You know best what you do. What you do creates your knowing. Please continue doing well and doing realistically. Judge yourself by your own reality-based standards.

Today it is raining. Whether I like rain or not, it is raining. Whether I want it to rain today or not, it is raining. Whatever my associations to rain, whatever my native language, whatever the recent history of drought or flooding; today it is raining. Just that.

Shakespeare wrote his thoughts about thinking; "Nothing is either good or bad except thinking makes it so. " Now I'll write my thoughts about Shakespeare's thoughts about thinking. I think he didn't go far enough. Perhaps only thinking about thinking about good and bad makes thoughts about good and bad. Whatever. My point is that our self-limiting obsession with word-thoughts sometimes distracts us from Something beyond words. On the other hand, words may invite us to go beyond the very word-thoughts to encounter that Something.

This wisp of awareness I call "me" appeared out of nowhere and now sometimes disappears during sleep. The questions of its origin and ultimate destination only appear when this awareness-me is present. When I am "gone", no questions or worries appear at all. To recall this truth brings relief to this-me-now, but it matters not at all to the me that is lost in sleep or work or play. What needs doing next is sometimes all there is.

If you believe that you can do anything then you aren't paying very good attention to reality. There is a great deal you cannot do. You cannot pay your bills by laughing at them, for example. You cannot turn anger on and off at will. You cannot prevent yourself from growing old or experiencing the occasional failure.
On the other hand, there is a great deal that you can do. You need not psyche yourself up or make a commitment or empower yourself or attain some mysterious enlightened power to do what you can do. You merely need to do it. After accomplishing something, then you know you could do it. Never before. So keep safely tucking your doings into the past. Thus you build confidence.

I'm unimportant. To the reader of these words I'm just represented by marks on paper. You are the most important person in your world. What you do results in vital changes to the world. Your doing keeps you alive. Your doing keeps these words alive. Thank you.

We can add so many interpretations and expectations that they interfere with our seeing plain facts. Involved in a discussion we can miss the car's turnoff exit. Anticipating a scolding we can miss gentler information in his voice. Raw perception may be impossible, but getting close may be useful at times.

The problem with obsessively checking and rechecking (to see if the gas and water are off, the stamps are on the envelope, the spelling is correct, the fly is zipped, email has arrived, buttons are buttoned, and so forth) is that the next task doesn't get done promptly. Uncertainty is unpleasant but unavoidable. So move from task to task.

Involve yourself in life. Notice, have purpose, act. Your life isn't nearly as complicated as you THINK. Simply live it, moment by moment.

My thoughts about you are not you. My memories of you are not you. My perception of you is not you. There is no way I can love you or hate you. How deeply I feel for these creations of mine! Meanwhile I eat and walk and work and play and sleep.

There is no winning or losing in life. There is no mind you can locate or see or touch or hear or smell or taste or fix. Yet certainly Something sees and hears. If we call it a mind we are already playing its game.

I didn't want to begin writing this morning. But now that I'm doing it, writing is just fine. The flavor of this candy is not exactly as I anticipated, but the flavor, too, is just fine as it is. What I expected went away somewhere, lost in what is this now.

Something offers you opportunities for action. Something evaluates those opportunities and sets your purpose. Something causes you to act in one direction or another (inaction is impossible; even sitting quietly is doing something). Something brings a result. This "you" shrinks and disappears. Where did you go?

We have many distractions available to us. We call them distractions because they have the potential of sidetracking us from our purposes. We may die at any time, so go straight toward your objectives.

Future hopes and past regrets are common elements of human thought. They can distract us and/or suggest what needs doing now. Use them wisely, then let them drift away replaced by the current current.

The only realistic way to check out the accuracy of these words is to test them in everyday life. Reality judges and responds to such life advice. Swim; don't try to float.

This morning I am sleepy. I have a number of stories about why, and none of the stories is related to when I went to bed last night. Even the latter tale fails as a believable story/explanation. I can't even tell you why I don't know why I'm sleepy.

Reality teaches us that rain is wet, that results aren't always as expected, that we can't outrun our past or future, that talking about changing our behavior is easier than changing it. The lessons from Reality come repeatedly in various forms. It's a good thing they do so because we forget them so frequently.

Pie in the sky is neither pie nor in the sky. You knew that. But the sky is not in the sky, and pie is not pie. Did you know that? Beware, a happy and peaceful life, loads of self confidence, and attaining enlightened power are also sky-less and pie-less fantasies. Many word games aim to keep people docile and self-content. I just want you to be realistic. Beware!

I don't have to play life by your rules. Yet I must be prepared to pay a price if I don't. That's just fine. Prices bring more rules, more possibilities, more purposes, more doing, another "this."

Clever talk is like an attractive oil painting. You can appreciate it, but you don't try to eat the abstract apples. One way or another we may try to represent those apples. Life comes in a variety of flavors.

Unconsciousness and blank minds solve very few real-life problems. Jumpy, unfocused minds are similarly ineffective. Ready minds are just that, ready. You can't get ready to be ready-minded. You are or you are not.

How I see you at any given time depends on you, but also on my mood, my recent past experiences, my immediate objectives, and so forth. This complex mix produced my perception of you. You, too, change in response to your perception of my perception of you. This change in you alters my perception of you and so on. Furthermore, these dynamic changes influence how I see myself. Questionnaires and interviews provoke the same sorts of feedback dynamics. However you respond to them is already wrong.

No one sees nothingness, though some may think that they do. Perceived nothingness is already coded as something. My vision of you is already coded as my vision; it is not you. No discipline allows one to be free of one's lenses. That is just fine. Lenses, too, are worth investigation. Note that investigating lenses requires lenses.

Words can stand for things I can touch--for example, this camera, this pen, and this zipper. Some words stand merely for other words. I can't put my finger on God or peace or a soul. Wisely avoid treating the second sort of words as though they were the first sort.

You can't understand mind or God or enlightenment or love in the same way you can understand a plastic bottle. All you can do with "God" is drape assorted word combinations about it. Anyway, you can drink from the plastic bottle.

The ability to recognize a gift is a gift. The ability to give a gift is a gift. The ability to see the truth in these words is a gift. The ability to recognize the ability to see the truth in these words is a gift. What is not a gift?

We tend to interpret in terms of our own convenience. What is in it for me? is a common trend in our evaluation process. Learning to consider the convenience of others (other people, other creatures, other things, other moments) broadens our perspective.

It is amusing to be called "Doctor," "Professor," "Sensei (in Japanese)," and "Sir." The words go away when I am alone, writing. It really doesn't matter whether these terms of respect are spoken sincerely or automatically, without thought. The words go away when I am alone, dying.

How can I "manifest" an ideal? What does it mean to "live out" one's principles? In what way do I "incorporate" wisdom in my daily life? Sometimes the words boil down to who is served first at the table, who goes through a door first, who takes out the trash, who eats that last cherry, whose hair is cleaned off the sink by whom. Then, knowing, somehow, that all those "who's" are somehow one makes a difference, too.

Laws are limits of last resort. We don't need laws about giving too much or listening too carefully or over-donating or offering too many smiles or offering too many apologies. Why is that? We do know what is right and what is necessary. Sometimes we just don't do what is right and what is necessary. By now perhaps we can dispense with fairytales about why.

No matter how long we talk together or live together I cannot see the world with your eyes. Yet the more time we spend together the more alike we seem to become. I find myself taking on some of the characteristics of my students. So think carefully about those with whom you want to associate.

Losing yourself in work, play, service, writing, painting, driving, whatever, changes subject into object. The dissolved self gets spread around as it expands to fill the current container.

Looking outside yourself for salvation is just fine provided you look far enough. Salvation comes moment by moment. You need not project some slightly larger than life image on a temple screen.

The more you desire something, the more anxiety you feel about failing to get it. The more you value something, the more anxiety you feel about the possibility of losing it. Desires are inevitable. So anxiety is inevitable, too.

"Understand" has many meanings. One kind of understanding involves words, properly placed in meaningful order. Another kind of understanding is intuitive and wordless. I can't really describe love or terror properly with words, but if you have experienced them, you know.

Did you realize that your greatest achievement is reading these words now? And then your greatest achievement will be what you do next, and then next, and so on. Anyway, you will forget about achieving as you get involved in your next doings. New you's require new achievements. Of course!

This you won't die. But some you will die. Count on it. So give that future you some worthwhile memories. Fearing death is just fine. However, remember it is not the death of you-now that you fear.

Most of the time you are too busy to think about words like heaven or hell. They are merely words anyway, attached to other words you read or heard. They are not attached to anything you ever experienced. If experiencing heaven or hell is actually possible you know what preparations need to be made. Then you can't report back about heaven or hell.

Reality responds directly to what we do. Put another way, Reality responds directly to what Reality does. Certainly, talking is something that Reality does. But Reality's response to talking varies.

"Paradise" is a fine word. So is "peace" as in "peace of mind". Have you ever seen these concepts? Don't let fine words distract you from keeping your shirt buttoned and your shoelaces tied.

I am just one way Reality gets its work done. Thinking of myself as a means, a living tool, a process fits my dynamic experience. The doing is important whatever turns out as a result.

You show up here and now with all you have, the whole package. To change your package change what you do. Then you become a new package. It is as easy and as hard as that.

I have lots of answers for you, more than one for every question. But you need my answers less than you need your senses and your muscles. My job is not to convince you but to offer intriguing, challenging words. The words don't really matter so much. You can't use them to improve your life! Do you understand why not?

Singing, whistling, and humming are sometimes pleasant noises, sometimes not so pleasant. I learned to sing some Japanese folk songs in English, but my translation may be strange and my voice is imperfect. Anyway, I sing. Or something sings me. Despite these varied lyrics of psychology do you recognize the tune by now?

"I have a lot of choices" means nothing. What specifically needs doing now? Abstract choices take wings and fly away. Abstract freedom flies away, too. Keep yourself grounded, even when sailing your mind.

Stringing words together is an author's job. We must be careful not to make word necklaces too tight and choke ourselves. We are all authors.

Once you catch on to these principles you can begin to anticipate the meaning of new Constructive Living (CL) talk and CL puzzles. When you get really good at CL you can forget CL altogether. Then you just accept and act. Be careful not to discard CL too soon, though.

Were you ever angry and wanted to tell someone off, but you knew you would be in trouble if you opened your mouth? Scold or swallow, either way you would suffer. Did you ever want to give advice but knew it wouldn't be received well? Sometimes no solution looks attractive. And that situation is okay, too. While suffering, go on with your life. What else can you do?

Life doesn't always work out as you hope or expect or deserve. However each moment turns out, you will keep on hoping and expecting and evaluating. While your mind keeps working, keep your body responding to what needs doing.

My head in the clouds, I tripped on the sidewalk crack. Are your dishes washed? Is your bed made? Is your laundry done? Are your bills paid? What needs to be done right now?

Mastering the vocabulary of a system of thought may be both rewarding and limiting. Don't let elegant words distract you from Reality. Keep on fitting yourself to Reality.

For all your hopes and dreams your life now is as it is. Reality responds to what you do and not to what you think or hope or dream. Actualizing involves action.

Our bodies are borrowed from our ancestors. How we maintain our bodies is up to us. Trading bodies is impossible. So get done what needs doing with what you have.

I cannot see or hear for you. I can only imagine what it is

like for you to see and hear. When I do that I surprise myself in more than one way. And I become more like you (or so I think). Thank you.

How far up can you climb? Can you perch for long on the heights? Don't be foolish. The ladder is spider web thin and rests on the ground.

This world is what we have to work with, including us. I can't offer you a better Reality or even an alternate Reality to the one that includes you. I can suggest that you redirect some of your usual self-focus toward what looks like something else or someone else. Losing yourself helps you find more of Reality than you thought existed.

You have preferences; so do I. Strong preferences are called addictions these days. You might be surprised how ephemeral preferences really are. Examine them by abandoning them now and then, while going on with your life. In more than one way slavery is stupid.

Reality sends things to do, and someone has to do them. Become the kelp in the breaking wave. Passive when necessary, active when necessary, become Reality's response to Reality.

Reality keeps coming. You can't hamper it or block its way altogether; it just flows around you (you as part of it, after all). So ride the stream alertly and well. What flowed past already is past. Even walking in running water is praiseworthy.

Where is your personality when you are asleep and not dreaming? Where does that entity you call you go? Your clothes and body and tools and words are all borrowed. So are your sensory inputs and thoughts. Borrowed from whom? From where?

I can guess and suggest what you might need to do. But only you know what you need to do. I must honor your knowledge and judgment while keeping clear what I need to do.

How do you know what needs to be done? You just know. If I offered you a book full of explanations it would be spectacles without lenses--useless however fashionable. Words are sometimes useful playthings, but they never quite touch Reality. Even these words.

Here is a box of tissues. But it's not really "a box of tissues." And it's not really "a pattern of sensory input" or "a tool for blowing my nose" or "a string of neural impulses in my brain." See? Right here. Now.

Sounds are morphed into meaning. Who morphs them? Who created meaning? Don't be fooled by these worded questions morphed into meaning.

Would these words make less sense if written on toilet paper? Would they seem more down-to-earth? Would you be less likely to think of them as noble or scholarly or classy? Whatever form it takes truth is truth. These words, however...

I'm on a train right now. I could be at a desk or on a plane or in a coffee shop, but I'm not. I could be writing poetry or eating a cookie or pondering future trips, but I'm not. I'm on a train right now.

Flipping back and forth between big ideas and a piece of chocolate candy is great fun. I don't regret either. Each has its place, but where is its place? Is this a big idea puzzle or a chocolate candy puzzle?

You must stay grounded or you will drift away into mind clouds. You must purposefully move your body or you will babble. You must climb or wilt. Pain is inevitable, but you must do or die. Then you will die anyway. Same word, many meanings. Drifting, drifting.

Life keeps changing. Life is so often unpredictable in its change. We would like something solid, something we could depend on constantly. Well, we have it. It is change.

Steady practice and habits bring some stability to life. Without an alarm clock my body wakes me very early each morning because it is my custom to get up early. We grow habits by nurturing them with repeated behavior. Familiar places and people and language bring some orderliness to life, too. But underlying all is change.

We make up stories for children about the tooth fairy, Santa, and the Easter Bunny. We make up stories for adults about personality, history, and society. Stories invite us to believe that we understand something that we don't understand. Be careful; you cannot become a child again.

Unanswerable questions promote undecipherable answers. If you approach a foolish question in a direct way and try to answer it straightforwardly, you will only add to confusion. Some questions must be challenged because they contain mistaken assumptions. An example is "What is the best way to control my emotions?" Any attempt to answer that question straightforwardly is wrong.

Meditation involves bringing attention back to some focus again and again. Attention naturally drifts from topic to topic. Practice can lengthen the period of specific focus. You might wonder who reminds you to bring back your attention when it has wandered away from your desired focus.

You can dissolve yourself in Reality. In those moments you are free from petty worries and complaints. You become just Reality's way of getting Reality's tasks done. When you disappeared this way in the past where did you go?

Perhaps you look for some magic words of insight. I offer only sidewalks and cabbage leaves and scissors.

You see with your eyes. What you see and how well you see and how much you really do see is up to you. How many times have you looked at the walls of your office or your home? Yet what details could you draw for me now of patterns of paint or framed pictures and posters.

Turning from now to now the past goes away, though its effects linger. Your sins and successes are washed away by the tides of time.

These days most people smile when photographed. The camera doesn't care whether they are happy or not. Can you say that they are happy? Can they say so?

You can't hear a "bell" or beat a "drum." Actually, some "bells" you can hear, but the sounds are just sounds until you add meaning.

For all our beliefs, hopes, and fears about death we know nothing about it except what we can observe from outside. Yet our minds chatter on about death, ignoring the fact of simply not knowing. I don't know if death brings something better than life or not. I do know that death prevents actions that might solve some of our problems. So it is better to act to solve problems before seeking possible escape or solutions in death.

I cannot control your anger, your fear, your dreams. I can suggest activities, point out behavioral options, advise about probable outcomes, and so forth. You remain responsible for everything you do. I remain responsible for everything I do. In this sense each of us is absolutely alone.

Your family, your company, your reputation, and your body arose from chaos and will disappear into chaos. Why do you work so hard? There are two good reasons. Do you know them? At bottom, they both have to do with debt.

When giving and receiving refusals, simply turn to what needs doing next. Life doesn't always conform to our convenience. Regrets are drags on behavior. Proper behavior eliminates regrets.

How do you know what needs doing next? Sometimes a request appears. To respond to a request in a sensitive, realistic fashion requires keen observation and a non-intrusive self. Spread yourself around.

However enlightened you may become, you will die. However rich or famous or athletic or careful or long-lived you will die. Sentences require punctuation. Craft your sentences well. Now, also.

You are not who you were yesterday. You are not who you will be tomorrow. Memories and dreams are neither who you were nor who you will be. You have only this you, now. This you is quite enough. Welcome.

Sometimes we think noble thoughts and remember wise sayings. Sometimes we recognize truth. Sometimes we act with enlightened purpose. Sometimes. Anyway, it is good practice to pay attention to our inner and outer surroundings.

There is no way to be good enough or thoughtful enough or enlightened enough or aware enough to earn what Reality presents us with moment by moment. No one merits this immediate salvation. Nothing is held back from us, whatever we might think. There is always exactly enough to make you you and me me.

Sometimes we may not want to look at the truth. Reality can be painful. But recognized or not, Reality is as it is. Lying to yourself or someone else won't change what bothers you, but always changes you.

What wakes you up from sleep? What causes you to recognize your name when called? What gives meaning to these words? If you answer "My brain" you are only partially right. Your brain didn't make up that answer all by itself.

Look behind my words. Look under them. Then throw them away as fast as you can. Then later on pick them up again and give them to someone else who might have a taste for them.

Your nostrils are wide enough to breathe. Your legs are long enough to reach the ground. Your mind is sharp enough to understand this sentence. What more do you want?

Translations can be better or worse than the originals. Clarifying muddy prose is an art, borrowed from Real experience. Keep checking words against experience to maintain a clear translation.

Windows both let in sunlight and reflect it at the same time. I'm a window. How well I do my job depends on how transparent I am at any moment. The light is always there.

We have stories about why we do what we do, but you

need not believe them. Even if the stories are created by professional psychologists they are not more than fairy tales. We can see what we do but not why.

A secret service is performed by doing a service without anyone knowing about it. No one will thank you. No one will know of your kindness but you. It is pure giving. It is particularly useful when performed for someone whom you dislike.

I have heard a lot of words over the years. Today I am on silence, no talking. So are the people around me at this retreat near Mt. Fuji. We learn about the value and danger of speech. Occasional periods of silence are worth your time.

There is a lot of foolishness going around dressed in religious and scholarly garb. If you put on such word clothing people may bow to you, but foolishness remains foolishness. Reality is much more impressive than we can describe verbally. Check out what you hear with your own experience.

If I said I was enlightened, would you be impressed? If I humbly said that I wasn't enlightened, would you be more impressed? What if I avoided the topic altogether? Now it's too late to avoid the topic. What to do...what to do...

You can't escape from your mind. I can't get into your mind. Each of us is ultimately alone. Yet we share this one Reality, however our perspectives on it may differ. In that sense we are not alone at all.

Time flies and drags. Fresh moments bubble up and are parsed into seconds, minutes, days, weeks, months, years, and so forth. Time seems to disappear when we are lost in some task. Then it pops up again when we finish. Where did time go?

Dawn arises this morning, and I can't find a moment when the sky changed from night to dawn. A feeling arises into my mind so gradually, so naturally. When was it not there?

Some folk you take to like family. With others you never feel comfortable. Is it them? Or you? Or both? Anyway, your behavior must fit not your feelings but rules of social courtesy and kindness. It is your responsibility to control your controllable behavior, whatever your feelings.

My thoughts grow old as I do. My feelings grow old, too. Rocks age; carbonation in bottles ages; air grows stale. Grab a handful of air and watch it grow old.

Risk is unavoidable. It's just a matter of which risks you notice and which risks you choose. Perhaps some of your basic assumptions are at risk when you read this book. Perhaps not. We are all daredevils in life.

We can talk about constructive action, but talking is not doing what we talk about. We can dream and plan and commit ourselves. We can determine and motivate and mentally rehearse and positively encourage. However, no one flies by flapping mental wings.

It takes a few days to settle into a new life routine or to fall back into old life patterns. We can monitor our behavior pretty well for a few days. Be careful to put forth best behavior on that first and fourth day. Start counting days every day.

I see myself as the main character in this play. You see yourself as the main character in this play. Everything else is a kind of prop. Who wrote the script and built the sets and stage? How can I be both main character and chief audience, too? The main character is in no position to objectively evaluate the script. Play your life well.

Earlier, someone wrote that Reality is as it is. Of course. And it still is as it is now, though different from what it was. Why bother to wish it were otherwise? Get on with your doing.

My experience of these surroundings is not the same as a detailed recording of these surroundings. My written words are not the words that come into my mind. My eyes don't see visual data. My ears don't hear record able sounds. Do you understand these differences? My mind can actually create sights and sounds that never were. It does so all the time. So does yours.

When you consider something to be holy, then you have categorized other things outside the holy box. When you want something a lot, other things become less desired. Who don't you love? What is not failure? Where are you not?

What really needs doing in your life? What must you do right away if you were to die tomorrow? Next year? I'm not asking what your spouse or parents or boss or children or clergy expect of you. Use your borrowed life well.

Waves of Reality keep coming whether you notice them or not. No philosophy offers you a breakwater. Recognize Reality's inevitability and keep swimming/surfing.

Someone changed our diapers and fed us before we knew the words "diapers" and "food." Someone cuddled us and clothed us before we knew how to say "thank you." Soon after we learned those words of thanks we hardly used them with our parents, if at all. We accepted others' service as if we had earned it. We still do. No one balances debts. No one stands alone.

Words help us organize our experience by highlighting and hiding. Reality is promoted and blocked. We think, talk, and otherwise act according to rules. Whether transcending these rules is possible or not, it might be useful to examine them. But how do you get off the road if you are the painted centerline? How can I get outside myself to see myself? Do you sometimes think you can?

This book, this pen, this page--Reality appears in concrete, specific form. Books in general come only in word/thought form. You may know about "all computers" but you can't touch them. So if you are worried about "what people might think" you are drifting in space.

Whatever you think of my words, go look at a flower, drink a glass of water, smell a hatband. Keep yourself grounded with occasional simplicity so that your mind doesn't sail too far.

Even computers can arrange words in interesting patterns. Understanding those words is something else again. Defining words and analyzing meaning with more words is bouncing around within the box. Boxes vary in size, but they remain boxes.

Planning a vacation is not going on a vacation. Wishing for an education is not getting one. Good intentions are not good actions. You have to move your body to get from here to there. Then you're at a new here with a new there in sight.

It's a good idea to make friends with your mind. Get to know it by spending time alone with it. Let it provide the distractions. You don't need books or television or alcohol or sports to wind it up all the time. Let it unwind in some quiet place. A close working relationship is useful in life. Hello, mind, how have you been lately?

Originality brings you extra credit on life's exam. Fresh senses and fresh connections dance forth out of nowhere. Look for the new angle, the unseen twist, the sharp discovery. Life is gleaming. Don't miss the backlit subtitles.

Love is a many-splintered thing. Pricks of jealousy and loss join doubts about worthiness and permanence. Don't let yourself be obsessed with love. Be ready to let go when letting go is necessary. The love may remain for a while, but the clinging must stop. You and love deserve better than fixation.

No hopes, no memories. How sad! Only hopes, only memories. How sad! Hopes and memories happen to you, like feelings and the weather. You can regulate them somewhat, indirectly, through what you do.

Did you ever wish a beautiful sunset would last longer? Did you ever wish a boring lecture would end sooner? Reality happens at Reality's pace. It isn't built solely for our convenience. Glean what can be gleaned from each moment.

Carrying around lots of mental baggage is tiring. A clear mind offers room for original thoughts to appear. Inspiration requires emptiness. How full is your mind cup already?

Consider yourself the main character in a movie. What is the title of the show? Everyone else is in the movie, too, fellow actors of a single film. Each actor sees himself/herself as the main character in the movie, this one single film. Who, then, is the audience?

Trying to grasp the breadth of the universe is futile. The mind won't stretch endlessly. Trying to grasp the tiny size of an electron is futile. The mind won't contract endlessly. We snack on metaphors as though eating a full meal.

Sometimes I see myself as though I were outside myself. I pretend such viewing is objective. Sometimes I "feel" self-conscious. I pretend such viewing is subjective. Sometimes only the traffic sounds and autumn colors happen. Objective and subjective go away.

What is there to open if I say I will open up myself to the world, to you? What was closed up before? The breeze was there all along, I suppose. How could it be shut out? What closed boundary separated the breeze and me?

You can't be wrong about what you like and dislike,

about what you feel, about what you need to do. But you can be wrong when talking about such things or implementing them. The safety of relativity and subjectivity is limited. Actions imply responsibility.

Today is exactly long enough for today's happenings. You are properly prepared to do what you need to do with just enough time to do it. You could ask for more, but you won't get it.

Walking down the street. Right foot step, left foot step. Right foot step, left foot step. Right foot step, left foot step. Going somewhere. Just walking.

When angry or tense or afraid we miss details of our surroundings. So focused on our enemy or our fear, we fail to see much else. Making an effort to see and hear (and smell and taste and touch) in such circumstances does what to the feelings? Check it out.

Some of our suffering is inevitable. We will feel pain,

grow old (if we don't die early), people will leave us, and so forth. Some of our suffering, however, we cause ourselves unnecessarily. Such unnecessary suffering has been called "suffering on top of suffering." Anticipated misery, remembered misery, resented misery, resisted misery--all are added to ordinary suffering by our misdirected mental processes.

Some sounds are more readily unlocked from their associations. Some visual illusions don't make sense at first. Nevertheless, it is not a good idea to try to abandon all associations. You want to know what is edible and what is not, for example.

Gifts are gifts whatever you call them. Gifts rain on us whether recognized or not. We might as well accept them, noticed or not, desired or not. All gifts have strings attached. Accept those strings, too.

Itches don't have to be scratched immediately. Pain doesn't have to be relieved immediately. Such messages of feeling should not be ignored, but other factors also need consideration before we act. You may have been taught that acting immediately on feelings is always a good thing; such action is said to "get the feelings out." Foolishness!

Life is as it is. Life is neither perfect nor imperfect. Neither is it as dreamed of nor as dreaded. It just is. Given that it is designed neither for you nor against you, what needs doing next?

Expectations help us make sense of the world. They also limit us by encouraging us to ignore information we don't expect to be relevant. Make effort at times to observe with fresh senses, with minimal expectations. Discoveries await you.

Do you want super powers? You can go beyond yourself without them. Become a mountain path, a rushing stream, a gas station pump. You know how to do so already. Just do it.

Science teaches us some of the how's, but none of the why's. I know something about how my mind works, but not why it exists at all. Yet it does exist. How kind of it!

I don't make rain or sunshine. I don't even "make" my thoughts about rain or sunshine. Those thoughts, these words, just happen. We say that they happen "to me," but that is just our way of talking.

Growing older I sometimes forget what I just did, why I'm standing in front of the cupboard, whether I visited that temple before. Every moment really is a fresh one with its fresh me.

Sometimes we must accept the unacceptable--a loved-one dies, a sudden illness hits us, a cherished plan falls apart. Sometimes we challenge what we know to be impossible. No problem there. Those mental contrasts are merely smoke-words. Just don't give up while giving up.

Wise discipline requires gentle toughness, kind severity. Sometimes you won't feel like doing what is right. The feeling is just fine, but do right anyway. Don't let feelings alone push you around. Reality deserves better.

Where do all your future dreams go during an earthquake or an auto accident? Something needs your attention right now. Always. That something may involve instant action or planning for the future. Whatever that something is, do it well.

Tales of bravery are not bravery. Prayers of action are not action. Dreams of progress are not progress. Don't be fooled! Merely talking about feelings and fixes solves very little, if anything. Talking is talking. Real change requires real change.

There is a time for action, a time for rest, a time for drinking something warm. Who decides the times for you? Who decides the times? Why are times decided?

Why do times appear? Why? Is this a time for questioning? Why?

For all of life's complications, there is only one thing you need to do now. Do you see it? Do you do it? That is all you need to do. It is both sufficient and remarkable. You are Reality's gift to Reality.

I don't offer you anything special. I drive an ordinary car in an ordinary way on ordinary streets. You do, too, though you may not realize it. Being ordinary doesn't make one special. And one need not be special to become ordinary.

Do you believe that mystical words will solve your problems? Not on your life! You know enough already to live life well. Why read on? Why not read on? I hope you enjoy these words. All words are mystical.

The Internet reminds me of how much I don't know. It inundates me with information, much of which I don't need. There is no way for me to grasp it all, no need for me to grasp it all. With so much information available there are some things I'll never understand. That's fine, of course. So is my desire to understand what can't be understood.

I love her and I don't. I don't want to die, but I don't want to grow old. I enjoy cold weather and I don't. I know I will die in a plane crash but I make plans for after landing safely. Minds don't always work logically, rationally.

With your head in the clouds your neck is stretched long for chopping. Fortunately, your feet remain on the ground. Get your senses back down to earth so you stumble less frequently. Don't miss Reality's performance. On stage now!

You don't need faith or courage or curiosity. They come and go like all mental phenomena. The twinkling feelings you do have are already quite sufficient.

Acknowledge them and get on with doing life well.

You are both saint and sinner, kind and unkind, honest and dishonest, beautiful and ugly, strong and weak. To acknowledge these contrasts is not to condone them. Nevertheless, it is a waste of your time and effort to work so hard just to live up to an inaccurate image. There are better reasons to do life well.

You can't smash a rock with a blade of grass. You can't fix your mind with talk. You can't build character by napping. You can't run fast on crutches. You can't go back to your childhood. Get real! That is enough.

I have no responsibility for what you learn. You have no responsibility for what I teach. You grow wisdom thanks to your own efforts and Reality's gifts. For all of my suggestions to you, I get no credit for your development in any direction. I do what I need to do. You do what you need to do.

Dilemmas are creations of the mind. They don't exist in Nature. Here is a river--cross it. Here is a refusal--accept it. Here is a cry for help--answer it. Life isn't nearly as complicated as you may think. Discover the one correct path this moment. Respond to it.

Damned if I do; damned if I don't. Sometimes our possible choices all point toward undesirable outcomes. Sometimes doing what is right will lead to punishment. Whatever outcome you foresee, go straight ahead with what needs doing. Whatever does in fact occur, will bring with it what you need to do next.

There are many ways of talking about truth. Some ways are immediately clear on the surface. Other ways require deep pondering. But talk is talk. Wash dishes and pull weeds.

You can explore your own depths and never hit bottom. The exploration alone deepens your project. Without solving the puzzle of you, respond to Reality's cues with purposeful action.

Who has the right to teach? Teachers surround you. You are a teacher yourself. Don't follow my lead. Lead on!

My sleeping bag fits into its stuff bag. I'm repeatedly impressed that such a big bag fits into such a small bag. You don't need to fit so many quotes into your memory. Live out what you already know. Studying and memorizing may be useful, but they may also be ways to run away from more important doing.

The certainty of some fundamentalist Christians and Buddhists and Moslems interests me. Their faiths are macro-programs interpreting all experience for them. I want you to trust your experience, not necessarily as I have described it. Believe as you do, and check out Reality.

Some sounds wake us up from sleep sometimes. Other sounds don't. Asleep becomes awake. No measure of brain waves can record this daily miracle. Brain wave changes may accompany waking, but they do not equal this miracle.

Mistakes are products of the mind. They don't happen naturally. Mistakes are said to occur when an ideal is compared with a real event and a certain kind of discrepancy appears. The real event is natural. The ideal and comparison are mental adjuncts. So is this analysis.

Here is an idea for you. No, it isn't. How could I give you an idea? Are ideas like boxes of candy? Could I take out one from my mind and present it to you as a gift? Where would you put it? Into your mind? How strange is our talking and thinking.

Masatake Morita, a famous Japanese psychiatrist, pointed out that the natural mind keeps moving along, but the troubled mind gets stuck or fixated on something--a worry or a fear or a desire or some such. So let your mind keep on running along from word to word and beyond.

What do we want to pass along to children? Has trigonometry been useful to you? How about the dates of historical events? Children may find it useful to learn the boundaries of the unknown and the unknowable. Do you?

I measure and judge in terms of me. For all my efforts to objectify this me, to measure or grasp this me, I expand beyond the tools and techniques available. How does one measure a fire with a ruler. It is more than the dynamic factor. It is the convergence of measuring and object that makes my task impossible.

Inexact though they are, we want to offer words of help, of comfort, of support, of praise, of love, of compassion. Words can be useful, however imperfect. So can we.

To know yourself fully is impossible, but still you know something about you. You know your tendencies, your triggers, your skills, your weaknesses. You know your history. You create a new you and a new history by what you do now. Your estimate of your tendencies and triggers and skills and weaknesses is updated by what you do now. So do now well.

Desires bring sorrow and joy, success and failure, hope and despair. Desires are just fine as they are. Taste life's sweetness and bitterness. While tasting, chew thoroughly, then swallow, digest, and move on.

What does it mean to "represent" something? Is a painting of Mt. Everest the mountain itself? Is an actor really the role he or she plays? Is my mother now a representative of the mother who fed me as a child? Do I now represent the me of my childhood. Do these words represent Reality? How close can I come to what is really real?

Look around. What do you hear? What do you smell and taste and touch? This sensible Reality keeps supporting you in the moments you deserve its support and the moments you don't. Yet you probably want more much of the time.

When lost in work or play we are both right there and gone. How can that be? Why do we best find ourselves when we lose ourselves? You solve this puzzle often every day.

To think "Now I am observing" is not observing. To think "Now I am properly listening" is not to listen well. To think "Now I am lost in this task" is not to be lost at all. It takes practice to lose yourself and not notice it, as in tennis or anything else.

Once Japanese speech was a jumble of meaningless sounds to me. Now that I speak that language I can't turn the sounds back into meaninglessness. Sometimes, however, if I tilt my mind a certain way, I can find a different meaning in those sounds. Creativity involves such mental tilting.

Who is really free? Such abstract freedom means nothing. Is anyone free from gravity's influence or governmental pressure or social constraints? Have I narrowed our consideration with this previous sentence or have I merely added more abstractions to delude us. Watch out for talk about freedom, peace, happiness, suffering, sin and salvation.

It would be foolish to tell people not to worry about dying. Yet most of the time such worrying is not a problem for us. We're too involved in life to think about death. It is a fact that whatever we do, we shall die. Facts are facts, but attention is attention.

You are in no position to evaluate my life. Neither am I in a position to evaluate yours. How odd, then, that we judge others anyway, as though our judgment were absolute and ultimate. Furthermore, we seem to raise our standards when judging others. Why do you suppose?

Someone taught us how to speak. Someone taught us how to think logically and evaluate and behave properly. Yet we praise ourselves for our successes and blame others for our mistakes. Who taught us that? What did we learn just on our own?

Opposites attract...debate. Agreement attracts cooperation. Recognition attracts associations. We are mentally magnetized.

Words stamped on a page may become stuck in your mind. Don't let the stickiness of words prevent you from living well. Whatever he or she said, unglue the words and move on.

Wrap your eyes and ears around Reality. Don't let these words get in the way. Do yourself upright. While breathing, look about you and really see. When earthquakes happen theoretical talk goes away.

It's fine to sleep when you sleep. But don't sleep when

you are awake. Shutting down puts your mind in imagination mode. Fiction flashes and you miss the real show.

If I do this, maybe he will do that. However, if I do that she will probably do the other. Then again if... Be clear that dreams are dreams. Doing is doing.

There is no doubt that this body/mind will die, whatever that means. This name will die, too, but who cares? Who? Because this mind/body lives now, wrap it up well on this cold morning.

We are all students of Reality. We learn from light and darkness and words, too. Cold and heat teach us. Rough and sharp and smooth offer us classes for learning. Don't daydream while important subjects are presented. Know where you are when in the classroom.

Worrying about what others might think is like sliding around on an oil slick. Firmer footing is available. Know your destination and stride toward it even if it moves about. People think the strangest things, and rarely notice you at all.

Of course, I believe I am right. So do he and she believe they are right. And we don't always agree. So who is really right? The correct answer is right down below us. Dig down to it and the disagreements melt away.

For all your reading and courses and education and degrees you cannot understand and predict your mind well. Sometimes it seems to have a mind of its own. Why is that? What is that unpredictable variable (or variables) which makes yourself a puzzle, even to yourself?

Self-analysis adds complication to an already complicated mind. When introspection interferes with proper action, then you know which should be put aside.

Grappling with abstractions is a hobby for some. Rock

climbing Reality is more likely to benefit you. Pay attention to your next move.

Don't try to fix the unfixable. Don't let the fixable go unfixed. Sometimes the only way to determine whether something is fixable or not is to attempt to fix it.

When you need to let go, let go. Everything is borrowed. You will return everything in the end anyway. So avoid foolish clinging now.

No one knows what cats and babies think. You cannot empty your mind or become a mental giraffe. Use what you have. Point to your realistic purpose and proceed.

Eternal is an infinitely long word composed of seven letters. No one really understands its meaning, but most people talk as though they did. Infinity is another such word. What's going on here? Can you actually fit infinity into eight letters?

We all have preferences. Wise people take into consideration the preferences of others as well as their own. Reality's preferences shouldn't be ignored. What are some of Reality's preferences?

What you do with what Reality presents to you is up to you. And whatever you do Reality inexhaustibly presents you with more. How marvelous! You may be exhausted, but Reality never is exhausted. entropy notwithstanding.

Failure is easier to accept when you're not obsessed with success.

Rejection is easier to accept when you're not obsessed with being loved.

Lack of recognition is easier to accept when you're not obsessed with leading. Fit yourself to your circumstances and see how life softens.

There are three ways to be ordinary. One is to know no

other possibility. Another is to choose to be ordinary while knowing various other possibilities. The third way is to forget the other possibilities while just being ordinary. None of these possibilities is easy these days.

Run to the edge of the cliff and stop on a dime. Do all you can, then leave it up to God or Fate or Reality to determine the outcome.

Don't be obsessed with leading or helping or owning. While aiming to control people and things you are the one controlled. Free yourself!

Let Reality happen. You actually have no other choice, but you may wish otherwise. You cannot even speed up or slow down Reality's play. Life happens at Reality's pace.

Accepting Reality as it is forms the basis for changing it. Pretending Reality was otherwise or ignoring it does not promote change. Acceptance doesn't equal passivity.

Improve yourself as you improve what is.

Trying to pinpoint now, I find it elusive. Trying to grasp my mind I find it escapes me even while being me. Okay, I give up. I'll just write and eat and rake leaves and thank and apologize as needed.

My mind won't go away at will. Whose will anyway? So, living with it, I am it. I might as well get to know it, accept it, and use it as it uses me. Thank you, mind.

There is Reality's work only you can do. You need not make a big deal of it. Just quietly go about doing it. The highest reward for your work is more Reality appearing with more than you need to do.

Showy humble behavior is not humility. Showy words of thanks are not gratitude. Showy asceticism is not asceticism. Showy religion is not religious. In moments of genuine attainment we forget the show and just do what needs doing.

We come and go with nothing into nothing. We must discover what is right to do and do it while we have the chance. Don't litter.

Reality isn't always as we wish it to be. Reality doesn't always make sense. The alternative is unimaginable. We can make do with what there is while changing it. Thank you, Reality.

Purposes are vital. Even trying to live without purpose is purposeful. So chose purposes that are doable (controllable by your action), confirmable (you will know whether you accomplished them or not), and specific (detailed). Such purposes set up life as a game you can win with some consistency.

Look about you. Reality is about you, is about you. Discoveries await you if you seek them or not. It is particularly hard to be bored if you keep your senses alert. No one does so all the time.

I cannot do for you what you need to do. You cannot do for me what I need to do. Even filling in for someone or exchanging tasks, the tasks get done differently. You put your stamp or everything you do. Tying your shoes, buttoning your shirt, slicing bread--all require your special touch. Then watch Reality respond to you.

Hope arises when you do well and success appears imminent. Confidence arises when you do well and you know it. Pride arises with well-earned praise. These feelings FOLLOWED the doing. Don't be misled.

Your successes and failures present you with something that needs doing next. Others' successes and failures also present you with something that needs doing next. How kind! Don't miss the show.

No one owns time. We all borrow it. Patience is uncontrollable, but waiting is controllable. Fit your pace to the needs of the moment.

Institutions are designed primarily for the convenience of authorities. Use them as necessary, but retain your independence. Cooperate as necessary, but retain your perspective.

Your mind can flow around obstacles or batter itself against them. It can wear down obstacles or wear itself out obsessing about them. Allow your mind to keep on flowing naturally.

Not doing is always doing. Not planning is a kind of planning. Not desiring is a kind of desire. Not present or absent, but both.

Rituals, like habits, may be useful or harmful. Consider where they come from and where they go. Familiarity is a lubricant, but what is your purpose? Where are you going?

Harmony implies conflict. Conflict requires a kind of

harmony. Neither is possible without the other, though one or the other may take prominence in any given moment. Both are useful.

Life presents many round trips, but you never return to exactly the same spot. Your grief may remind you of childhood grief, but it is not childhood grief reemerging. Past feelings are all gone forever.

Appearances may deceive. However, appearances may be the only information you have without personal experience. Take time to investigate before make a long-term commitment. Commitment means dependable behavior, not consistent feelings or thoughts.

Summer--a cool breeze just blew in on my hand-- just enough.

Explanations can be useful (as in science), or meaningless (as in psychoanalysis). Words can be helpful (as in conference translations), or harmful (as in religious pronouncements). Don't let words get in the way of being realistic, even the words "being realistic. "

You have in mind general notions of what it is to be a good person, a   realistic person, an admirable person, a mature person, a kind and giving person, and so forth. Alongside these notions you have your everyday life with eating and reading and climbing stairs and fluffing the pillow and so forth. Check out the fit between these two sets. If the fit is not snug something needs to be revised.

Give a name to something and it comes into existence for the mind with that label attached. Misery, failure, neurosis, symptom, disaster, hopeless, and so forth are such names. What really exists is a happening or experience. Labels give us a handle on reality, but the handle can be stiff and hard to turn. We may be stuck with a perspective that is unrealistic and harmful. Examine your labels to determine their validity, reliability, and usefulness.

You are never alone, even when you think you are. At this moment a pen is one of my companions, quietly cooperating with my purpose. This book is cooperating with you. It represents papermakers, printers, publishers, booksellers, sales people, advertisers, and others only you know. Thank you.

Falling snow looks beautiful or troublesome depending, perhaps, on whether you carry a shovel or not. Even respected and admired people are imperfect. Imperfect is all right, just as it is. Perfectly imperfect. So is disappointment and disillusionment.

If you wish for autumn in springtime you will be disappointed. If you wish for summer in wintertime you will feel regret. Let winter be winter and spring be spring. Feelings, too.

A famous Japanese psychiatrist once said, "When climbing a mountain it is all right to give up as long as your feet keep moving upward." Giving up to your exhaustion, despair, and weakness is fine, so long as you keep on doing what needs to be done, rest or not. You discover then that giving up is a kind of game your mind plays. You get to make the rules of the game.

Knowing how to string words together in recognizable ways is not the same as knowing how to touch type or pass a football accurately. Knowing what needs doing next is not the same as knowing how to tap dance. Knowing what you prefer and knowing what you feel are yet other kinds of knowing. "Knowing" is one word with lots of meanings...be careful.

Some valuable gifts you can give others include your ears, detailed information, your experience-based advice, an introduction to valuable knowledge, and your time. We are privileged when allowed to offer such gifts.

Compare what you hear from so-called mental health experts with your own experience. Confidence follows success, it need not precede it. You can ask for a raise even while feeling shy or uncertain. Your feelings are not the most important part of your life. You cannot control your feelings. Do these statements make sense to you?

While driving to Dallas you don't want to keep Dallas in the front of your mind all the time. Accidents happen that way. On the other hand, to completely forget your destination results in confusion and missed turns. Sometimes this, sometimes that. Sometimes here, sometimes far away. Nevertheless, there is only here, now. Visions of progress are fine, but the execution of ideas requires attention to detail. While gazing at the mountain scenery, don't drive off the road.

Our minds tag things and events with all sorts of associations. I like x; I don't want y; x is pleasant; y is frightening; y ought not to be; I wish x were happening now instead of y. An alternative tag is z--this is the way it is. The other tags may still matter in the background, but the z tag focus is quite useful. Meanwhile, can you sweep the dust from your soul? Can you discard the accumulated rubble of your past? Can you remove your mind's burden of obsessions and fears? Each moment you are presented with a fresh mind. It is a gift. Have you noticed your new treasure? Did you thank it?

Talking about your project won't finish it. Dreaming about that college degree won't obtain it. Wishing for a loving partner won't attract one. Regretting one's past won't erase it. Denying one's faults won't eliminate them. You know all that.

You can read hundreds of books about how to live well. You can fill your mind with advice and techniques and noble thoughts. All such effort is useless compared with putting one constructive path into practice in daily life. Life is actualized through action. Doing gets something done. Life is as simple, and as difficult, as that.

Money and possessions both simplify and complicate life. Knowledge has the same capability to simplify or complicate life. Use what you have well. It is all borrowed, on temporary loan.

Science doesn't try to explain why causes have effects. Scientists look at specific effects and their causes. What causes fresh moments and meaningful thinking is still a mystery. For all the talk about brain activity and brain chemicals, no one knows how I created this sentence.

Some people seek deep philosophies of life before mastering face washing, bed making, room cleaning teeth brushing, dishwashing, their work, their play, and other aspects of daily life. Abstract words allow them to flee from everyday life activities. Master the basics first.

Meaningless questions can't be answered meaningfully as they are. Examples are: How can I manage my emotions? How can I bring out hidden feelings? How can I attain constant true happiness? Often, the best reply to such questions is laughter.

As you work toward self-development and personal

growth you have already succeeded. As you examine your life to make it more realistic, it already is. The end is in the doing, too. Make no mistake about it.

For all our hopes and dreams, life is as it is. For all our interpretations and insights, life is as it is. Recognizing this truth, what needs doing now?

Your image of me is not me. Your evaluation of me is not me. What I have written here is not mine. If all is borrowed, who is the borrower?

For all my writing I can't change your life. Word after word, I offer you my best words, but they are merely pointers. Commentary about the game is not the game itself. Do your best.

Who will follow you in the work you do? What can you pass on of value to those who succeed you? What life wisdom in what form will you leave for others? It's not too late to say or write something. It's not too late to model behavior as a gift.

Dirty floors need to be cleaned. Vegetables need to be peeled and chopped. Cars need to be serviced. Gardens need to be weeded. People and other living creatures and things present their needs to you. They need you. What needs doing next?

If you add or take away from this 365-day list is it the same list? If you substitute items in this list then whose list is it? We could spend time working on definitions, more words about words. Perhaps you could find better use for your time.

You are who you are. You are the perfect embodiment of you. It's fine to work to improve that you. The working-on-improvement you is just another perfect embodiment of you. Any result of that effort is, again, the perfect embodiment of you. Failure, too.

The ability to respond to life is a gift. Responding brings

new life. One way or another you always respond to life. You are part of life's response process.

When giving a gift, your heart need not be full of love and appreciation. When offering thanks, you need not feel grateful. When apologizing, you may or may not feel remorse. Anyway, do what is right to acknowledge a favor received or a trouble caused.

Watch yourself now and then to keep a check on your behavior. However, don't let the watching interfere with the doing. If self-consciousness is a problem, then watch yourself watch yourself. Then watch yourself watching yourself watch yourself, and so on until you get tired of the whole game and get back to doing.

When you make a mistake, just turn to what needs doing next. You change immediately from mistake-maker to next-doer. You have, then, no time to become severe-self-criticizer.

You don't put gloves on your feet or socks on your ears. You don't try to write with a sausage. So why do you try to figure out every angle when immediate action is required? Misuse of the mind is a common cause of unnecessary suffering, is unnecessary suffering.

Dwelling on past mistakes and successes can interfere with what needs doing now. The one who failed and succeeded then is not this you now. This you now is infinitely more valuable to the world at this time.

Life presents you with lots of possibilities for action. Imaginative action is always possible, even amidst routines. Discover new ways of doing in response to new discoveries through new noticing.

When someone else mistreats you or scolds you or ignores you they give information about what needs to be done. Do what is right. If they repeat their behavior just do what is right again.

You view advertisements with a certain degree of skepticism. Any string of words deserves the same distanced consideration. Religious, legal, philosophical, and psychological words are all suspect. They are lodged in word reality. So are these words.

You can't hold on to happiness or joy or faith or confidence or satisfaction or peacefulness or any other mental state. You can't preserve your desired self-image. Give up and let go of yourself giving up and letting go. What needs doing now?

You can't lift a bag of groceries with your mind. You don't travel to Japan with good intentions alone. Deciding to move is not moving. Committing yourself to give up tobacco is not giving up tobacco. Doing is doing; there is no substitute.

Honored or disgusting, all of reality is real. You cannot successfully focus on beauty and ignore ugliness. A life of good feelings only is impossible. Accept the whole of it, including the good and bad in you. Then work to change what needs changing.

You have a name, but it is not you. You have a job, but it is not you. You have a body, but it is not you. You have a family, but it is not you. What/Who are you?

Do I deserve to be where I am now? Did my actions earn me this place? Is this life a reward? Is it a punishment? Silly speculation. Life just is. Now what needs doing?

No salvation lies in silence. No salvation lies in speech. Examining the word "salvation" merely covers it with more words. It is better to bury it with behavior. What needs doing now?

We all have responsibility to pass on wisdom words to others. At times we can do so directly. At other times we defer and refer to others better able to communicate wisdom words. Wisdom is verifiable by experience.

There are lots of ways to wash dishes--while smiling, while grumbling, while thanking, while cursing, thoughtfully, carelessly, and so forth. There are lots of ways to avoid doing dishes, too. Unwashed dishes remain so until washed.

Your life keeps telling you about your life. Listen to it. My words about your life are of little worth compared to your life's teachings. You know what has worked for you and what has not. Be realistic.

No one imparts wisdom. I can't give you a wisdom present. I pass along words from my life experience. Something else generates wisdom in us. That something is worth searching for and recognizing.

We talk as though minds move from topic to topic, as though minds flow. But minds don't move in any geographic sense. The "movement" of minds is unique. Thoughts appear in sequence, then disappear. When called up again, the thoughts are not the same thoughts we had in the past. Each thought, each feeling, is new.

Thinking about thoughts is an interesting endeavor. Analyzing thoughts piles thoughts on thoughts. Thought mountains sometimes collapse under their own weight. Then we may just do what appears that needs doing.

Attempts to paralyze the mind with mind exercises are fruitless. Let your mind wander about on its own. It always returns home. No one ever lost his or her mind.

There is more than one way to get where you need to go. Don't be so fixated on one way that you don't see other routes. Don't be so fixated on looking for alternative routes that you fail to move forward on one of them.

I can't live your life for you. Neither of us wants that impossibility. Doing my life well is a full-time task, only sometimes successful. How about you?

If you aim to line up your thoughts and feelings in proper

order before doing what needs doing, you will rarely if ever get around to proper action. Without confidence or courage or certainty or compassion, just do what is necessary straightforwardly.

Don't get the idea that you are a sad person or a clever person or a happy person or a good person or a frugal person. You are a changeable person; sometimes this, sometimes that. Psychological tests and psychiatric diagnoses make you look like a statue. You are not a statue.

Do you wait for others to greet you first? Do you sit passively waiting for Fate to bring you a life partner or a lottery win or a relative's estate? While waiting, give life a "Hello" and get moving on some project.

Why are you reading this book? I'm sure you can answer this question, but if you thing a short while, you can give at least several alternative answers. Which one or combination is correct you don't know. These motivation stories are tales we learned to offer when asked why we do what we do. Anyway, we do what we do.

For all my presumed self-knowledge seasons come and go, people come and go, my eyesight comes and goes. Changes never end. I'm glad there is a now.

Minds drift and play. But keep your eyes on the road and off the mobile phone while driving. Listen when listening and focus when inspecting. Flexibility is not limitless.

Precisely what comes next no one knows. You can predict sometimes with more or less accuracy, but you never KNOW. So be alert, observe, respond, realistically. Here comes that next moment. Do life's tea ceremony at the pace Reality presents.

Do you hold on to some memory of past success or past love? Do you cling to a grudge? Do you resent your history, your race, your body, your company, your spouse, your parents? The past is gone, unchangeable. There is no need to drag it wrapped around your ankles, hampering your movement now.

If your aim is to be ever peaceful, without worries, blissfully calm, then your aim is off target. Aim for acceptance of worries, doubts, pain, grief, and anxiety as well as those pleasant feelings. You can hit that target at least some of the time.

Planning to exercise more and eat less won't cause you to lose weight. Hoping for a salary increase or a stock gain won't make you rich. Wishing you were smarter or taller or famous or fearless or successful won't bring your desires into reality.
You know that.

Give your mind a break by moving from purpose to purpose. A change of pace is a form of rest. You can send your mind on vacation with a book or video or film. Where does it go then?

Reality needs you. There are tasks only you can do. There is genuine satisfaction when you find those tasks and accomplish them. You are Reality's way of getting Reality's work done. What needs doing now?

Examine questions carefully. They all hold seeds of their answers. So foolish questions with foolish assumptions require foolish answers. Do you follow me?

In one sense, the less you think you know, the better. I'll challenge some of what you think you know already until you know little enough to learn more. There is a lot for us to learn and unlearn and relearn and unlearn and...

We are Reality's servants. We are also Reality's creators. How can we be both? Scrub your bathroom sink and see.

Maybe you would like a set of principles, an organized philosophy, to take home with you. You could put this book on the shelf alongside others and compare them now and then. I'm sorry to disappoint you. Ideas don't fit on a shelf. Here comes another one!

Right now I like warmth, sitting in a car in wintry Japan. Last summer I liked ice cream. My preferences keep changing. They fit situations and circumstances. Not only my preferences are embedded in circumstances. I am situated.

We make guesses about what will come next. We employ weather forecasters and stock market analysts and physicians. Then what comes, comes. That is just enough, just right, and just as it is.

You are on your own. Yet you partake of everything. You do your own life while supported by others. You rate full credit yet no credit, confidence without pride.

Does some of this writing make sense to you some of the time? Any response is fine.
I write in your mind's native language.

Your mind makes up stories about all sorts of things. Close your eyes and recall the painting nearest you now. Your mind may fill in colors and objects and arrangements not in the painting at all. Your mind wants to make sense of the world, but only a certain limited kind of sense. Keep an open mind about it.

New situations keep arising. You can fake your way through some of them by pretending to repeat previous actions. However, if you aren't clear about your purposes, some of the new situations will catch you offering unfitting behavior. Why does this behavior need doing now?

Here is some news: If you eat too much and exercise too little you will become fat. If you are not eating while reading these words you are cured of overeating. If you are not dead while reading these words you are alive. Good news! Of course, you neither live forever nor find yourself cured forever, but now, now...

You have stories about where you have been, what you did. You have stories about where you will go, what you will do. Nice stories are, nevertheless, only stories. They are compacted into words so you can think about them and tell others about them. But your trip to Washington and your childhood trauma and your graduation were not the same as the word arrangements you now have about them. However and wherever they are coded away you cannot re-experience those past events. Now is all you really have.

Somehow, this me seems to keep going, to keep on experiencing fresh moments. The moments are digested and turned into words such as "I just typed that last sentence" and simplified images. I am this cutting edge that appears to be moving forward through time, always experiencing/transforming, or so I remember it. Knowing this truth, I then disregard it and treat my memories as real and make future plans. This strategy seems to work much of the time, or so I remember it.

We can talk philosophy all day, but it won't get the lawn mowed. Talking philosophy is acceptable if the grass isn't high somewhere else.

What benefit could there be in comparing the reality of me with someone's ideal? I am this age, this height, this weight, this race, with this personal and educational history and these talents and limitations. Where do I go from here?

"What should I do?" the student asked me. "How should I know what you should do?" I replied. "I'm not you." "How profound!" the student remarked. I laughed.

As we grow older our bodies need more support. Something provides that support. Imperfect and undeserving, we are supported.

I don't remember names and faces of many people I met in 2000, but my fingers are cold as I write this morning.

Truth remains truth, whether or not I notice or remember it.

Don't go far away into the land of dream talk unnecessarily. Don't let word tickets get you on a train to nowhere. Stay clear on where you want to be now. Keep on track.

Anticipated or not, an event is as it is. Remembered or not, an event is as it is.
Dreaded or memorable, wonderful or terrible, whatever happens, happens. Accept it.
Merge with it. Then do what needs to be done about it.

Do you want to hear that life is mysterious, magical, and holy? Well, it is, and it is not. Those appended qualities are both present and absent in spit, buttons, tissues, gloves, shadows, balconies, neighbors, cats, riverbeds, digestion, and much more. There is no need to list everything.

Self-criticism is fine. Self-doubts are fine. Worries are fine. Fear is fine. So are flowers and birthday gifts and tasty meals. Look straight at them all, just as they are.

Life waits around somewhere as we sleep. Then it pops up again as we wake up. Running away from life by sleeping has that peculiar disadvantage. We don't wrap the holiday gift while sleeping.

While alive, sometimes you will be comfortable. Sometimes not. Life is like that.
What is the alternative?

First you learn possibilities. Then you practice these possibilities. Then you forget the possibilities while retaining the practice. In life doing is what matters. Pills don't teach doing.

Seeing requires both object and eyes. What your eyes see depends on your ability to focus. The contents of this package are varied. Open it up and see. Perhaps your focus will improve.

Up close and personal we observe certain details. The rest of the world disappears from our focus. Noticing always involves ignoring. Giving always involves causing trouble. Living always involves dying. Learning requires forgetting.
Understanding requires letting go.

I don't know what is in your mind. I can't get inside your mind, wherever that is. We can talk about the contents of our minds, but the talk isn't the same as the contents. Don't be fooled!

I'm not dead yet. This living me hears the traffic sounds and sees the frost on the window. There is no dead me here to worry about.

Let's imagine that everyone is looking at you. Now let's imagine that everyone is concerned with personal matters, taking no notice of you. Now let's consider the possibility that only the powerful and attractive people are watching you. Playing such foolish games we fail to see sunsets and oncoming trains.

Dogs and keys and cupcakes come to your mind. You don't go out and corral them. How kind of them to appear to you, only when you notice!

I don't know about wisdom. I'm certainly not wise. I know a little about computers and chocolates and words. Usually I trust chocolates.

Measure people by what they do or don't do. Measure truth by reality. Measure words by their fit.

Don't do what doesn't need doing. When in doubt, do something else temporarily. What causes you to know what needs doing? Information is only part of the answer.

No one needs to teach you how to be warm or cold, how

to be hungry or full, how to be angry or happy. What gifts they are! Accept them with thanks, grateful or not.

When your mind feels cluttered, hyperactive, or sluggish, you might try sitting in a quiet place attending to your breathing. Easing the mind's burden can be called "lightenment." Or go out for a walk.

You believe what you believe. You doubt what you doubt. You love whom and what you love. Making up stories about why won't change your preferences. New facts may change your preferences. But what is a fact?

You are the most important person in the world, to you. No matter whom you respect or love or fear you remain the central character in your life play. You decide what that central character does. Act well.

Not knowing is not the same as being ignorant. Knowing what you don't know is intelligent. Pretending to know what you don't know is regrettable. Many social scientists and clinical psychologists and psychiatrists and mental health counselors actually believe that they know something that they don't really know. They try to put water in a bucket made of water. It is just fine to not know.

Maybe you think that some of the words in this book need to be rewritten differently, that I am simply wrong. Thank you.

Without knowing everything about everything, without certainty regarding outcomes, I must act. To fail to act is to act. Sitting doing nothing is not doing nothing.
The question is always "which doing needs doing?"

What others do may not make sense to you, but it usually does to them. What you do may not make sense to others, but it usually does to you. Even if you tell others the meaning of your behavior, they won't understand it as you do. You are ultimately alone in your world of meaning. Yet we all share the same reality.

Where do fresh moments come from? Where does meaning first arise? Why do we ever know what needs doing? What is death? What is the connection and disconnection between this me and this brain? Even if you knew the answers to these questions could you communicate the answers to others? Meanwhile, the water is boiling and the dust is accumulating. What needs doing now?

The End

Manufactured by Amazon.ca
Bolton, ON

39207578R00059